Ellie Meets Her Stepdad

By Randall Hines

Ellie Meets Her Stepdad

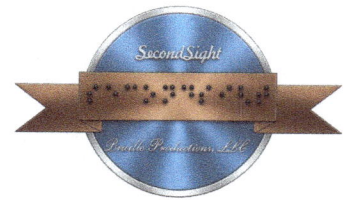

Copyright © 2025 by Randall Hines

ISBN: 979-8-9938323-3-3

Published by SecondSight Braille Productions LLC
www.secondsightbraille.com

Mom Tells Ellie About Her New Friend

Ellie had always thought it would just be her and Mom forever. For as long as she could remember, it had been that way — the two of them sharing breakfast at the kitchen table, cuddling late at night when Ellie couldn't fall asleep, laughing at silly TV shows while wrapped in the same blanket. Ellie was eight now, and she loved how steady and simple life felt with just the two of them.

But one day, Mom sat her down on the couch, her face soft and careful. "Ellie," she said, "I want to talk to you about someone special."

Ellie's stomach twisted.

Mom continued, "His name is Adrian. We've been seeing each other for a while, and I'd like you to meet him."

Ellie stared at her lap. She didn't like the idea of "someone special." Wasn't Mom's someone special supposed to be her?

The First Meeting

Adrian came over to pick them up that Friday to take them to dinner and a movie. He said they were going to watch whatever Ellie wanted to see. Ellie sat at the table with her arms crossed. He was taller than Mom, with kind eyes and reddish hair. He brought flowers for Mom and gave Ellie quarters for the arcade games at the movie theater.

"Hi, Ellie," he said warmly.

"Hi," Ellie muttered, not looking at him.

They ate Mexican food, her mom's and her favorite. Adrian asked Ellie about school, her favorite subject, and what kind of games she liked. Ellie answered with one word each time. She didn't want to give him the satisfaction of thinking she liked him.

When dinner ended, they went to the movies. Ellie seen them holding hands and did not like it. She reached over and took the hand Adrian was holding and held it. He wasn't acting like a guest — he was acting like he belonged. That made her chest ache in a way she couldn't explain.

The Weekend Outing

A week later, Mom suggested they all go to the park. Ellie wanted to say no, but Mom looked so hopeful. So Ellie dragged her feet all the way there.

At the park, Adrian tried to race her, and play games. Ellie rolled her eyes. She didn't want to play with him. She just wanted her mom. He did throw her the football, and she was amazed at how far he threw. Her eyes lit up.

She threw it, and it fell short of where she had wanted it to go. Adrian didn't laugh. He just showed her how to hold it, how to angle her wrist. After a few tries, the ball went soaring. Ellie's heart did a little flip — but she quickly crossed her arms again. She wasn't about to let him think he was winning her over.

Little Annoyances

Over the next few weeks, Adrian was around more often. He and Mom cooked together, laughed at jokes Ellie didn't get, and Adrian even hung stuff up in Ellie's room.

Ellie noticed changes. Her spot next to Mom on the couch wasn't always open. Her bedtime stories sometimes had to wait because Mom was finishing a conversation with Adrian. And sometimes, Mom would even let him pick what they all would eat and watch on TV.

She didn't like it.

"Why can't it just be us again?" she asked one night as Mom tucked her in.

Mom brushed Ellie's hair back. "Because I care about Adrian. And I think, in time, you might care about him too."

Ellie turned her face to the wall. She didn't believe it.

A Bad Day

One afternoon, Ellie came home from school upset. A girl in her class had made fun of her drawing, and the teacher hadn't noticed. She stomped into her room, slammed the door, and threw her backpack on the floor.

A soft knock came a few minutes later. "Ellie? It's Adrian. Can I come in?"

Ellie wanted to say no. But something in his voice wasn't pushy, just gentle. She shrugged, and he stepped inside.

He saw her drawing crumpled on the floor and picked it up carefully. "This is really good," he said.

"No, it's not. Everyone laughed at it."

Adrian sat on the floor beside her. "When I was your age, I tried to draw a horse once. It looked more like a lopsided dog. I was so embarrassed. But you know what? I kept trying, and eventually I got better. Don't let one person's words stop you from doing something you love."

Ellie blinked at him. No grown-up had ever admitted to being bad at something before.

That night, she redrew her picture.

Small Steps

Things didn't change overnight, but Ellie began noticing little things.

When Adrian came over after she was home from school, he always asked how her day was and really listened. Sometimes he would even bring candy. When she had trouble with her math homework, he showed her a trick to make multiplication easier. He would even let her get on his shoulders so she could touch the ceiling!

Still, Ellie clung to her stubbornness. She worried that if she liked him too much, it would mean she didn't love Mom the same way anymore.

The Big Argument

One Saturday, Adrian suggested they go bowling. Ellie groaned. "Do we have to? I don't want to go."

"You might have fun," Adrian said.

"I won't," Ellie snapped. "Why do you keep trying to act like my dad? You're not my dad!"

The words hung in the air, sharp and heavy. Mom froze, her face falling. Adrian looked hurt but calm.

"You're right," he said softly. "I'm not your dad. I'd never try to replace him. But I do care about you. I'd like to be someone you can count on."

Ellie stormed to her room. She didn't come out for hours.

Later, Mom sat on her bed. "Sweetheart, I know this is hard. I know it feels like things are changing too fast. But loving Adrian doesn't mean you stop loving me. And it doesn't erase what you've had before. It just means we can build something new."

Ellie didn't answer, but her heart squeezed.

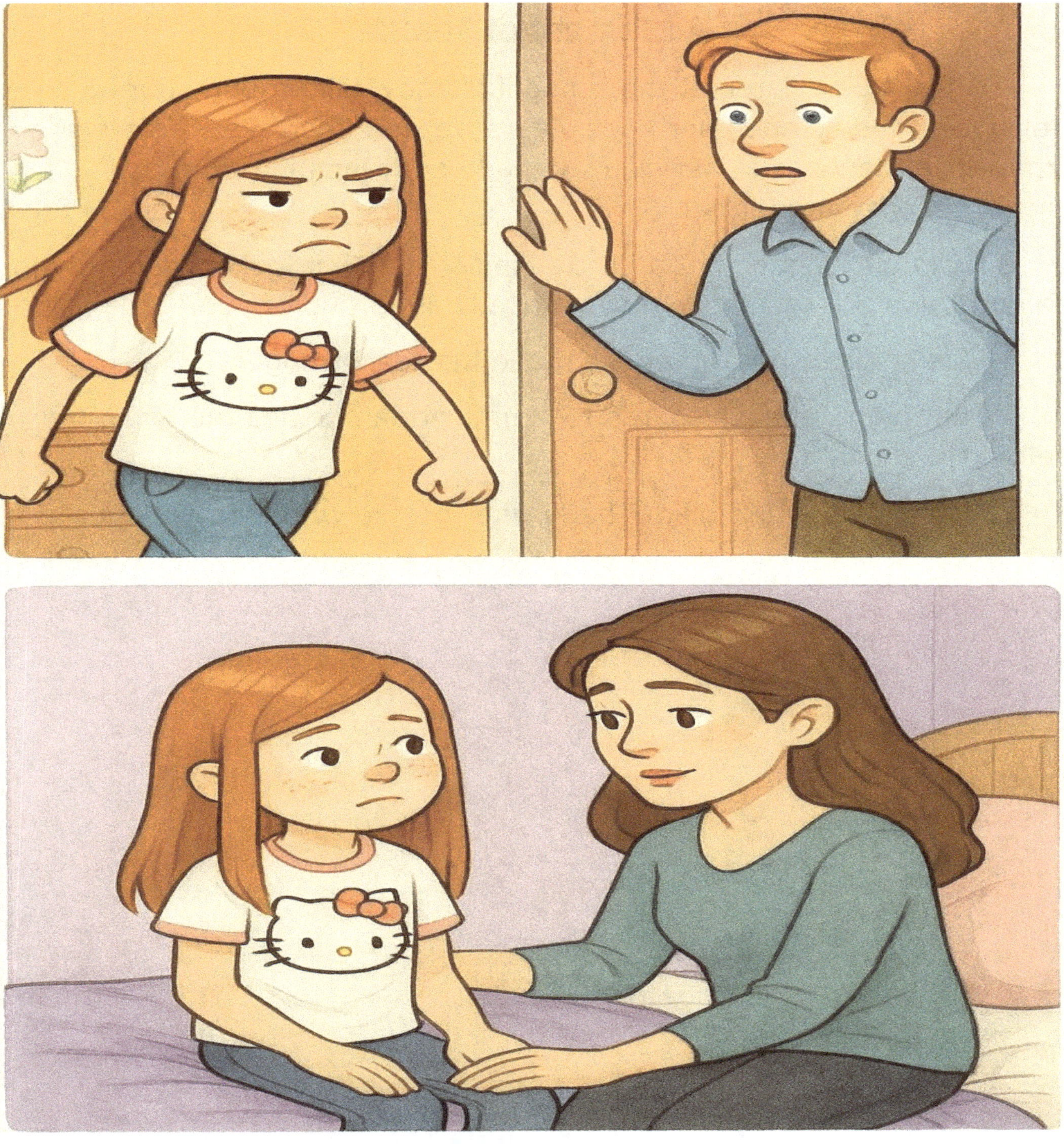

A Moment of Rescue

A few weeks later, at the school field day, Ellie tripped during a relay race and scraped her knee. Tears welled in her eyes. Before she knew it, Adrian was at her side. He had been watching from the sidelines, cheering for her.

He knelt, handed her a tissue, and said, "That looked like a tough fall. But you got up fast — that's brave. I am proud of you."

Ellie sniffled, but the praise made her feel stronger.

That night, she whispered to Mom, "Adrian helped me when I fell."

Mom smiled. "I'm glad. That's what people who care about us do."

Growing Closer

Over the next few months, Ellie slowly let herself relax around Adrian. They built a cardboard dollhouse together. They played with slime. He would chase her around, and even helped her not be afraid to swim in the deep end of the pool.

One rainy afternoon, Ellie found herself curled on the couch between Mom and Adrian, watching a movie. She realized she hadn't worried about sitting next to him — it just felt natural.

The Family Talk

One evening, Mom sat down with Ellie and Adrian. "I want you to know," she said gently, "that Adrian and I are planning a future together. That means he'll be around a lot. But Ellie, your feelings matter most to me. I want us to be honest about them."

Ellie looked at Adrian. For the first time, she didn't feel like he was taking something away. Instead, it felt like he was giving something — extra laughter, extra help, extra love.

"I guess ... I don't hate it anymore," she said quietly.

Adrian chuckled. "That's progress."

The Turning Point

The real change happened slowly. Ellie got more comfortable around him, and he was always with mom and her. He even got her signed up for gymnastics! She had been wanting to do that for a long time.

Adrian started a new thing round the house where Ellie would earn this fake money for her chores and then every Sunday after church mom and him would set out a bunch of toys like a store. She would have to decide what things she could get, and sometimes she only got one thing and saved the rest of her money until the next week.

She didn't want to admit it, but now that Adrian was with them ... she didn't want him to leave.

A New Beginning

By the end of the year, Ellie couldn't deny it anymore: Adrian was part of her life. She still had moments of doubt, moments where she wished it was just her and Mom. But more often, she felt glad he was there.

On her birthday, Adrian surprised her with a scrapbook of all the things they'd done together — pictures of the dollhouse, them swimming together (even though she'd frowned in that one), pictures of them playing with their dogs Bullet, Max, and Remy, and the time she got her ears pierced.

Ellie flipped through it slowly, her heart swelling.

When she got to the last page, she saw a note in Adrian's handwriting: *"I may not have been here for the beginning of your story, but I'd be honored to be here for the rest."*

Ellie looked up, her eyes stinging. For the first time, she wrapped her arms around him in a hug.

"Happy birthday, Ellie," he whispered.

And for the first time, Ellie thought maybe "stepdad" wasn't such a bad word after all.